LOVE

THE GREATEST POWER EVER KNOWN

The Addition of Faith Revolutionizes the Power of Love

ALFRED CHERUBIM

Love: The Greatest Power Ever Known
The Addition of Faith Revolutionizes the Power of Love

Alfred Cherubim
2024 © by Alfred Cherubim

All rights reserved. Published 2024.

BIBLE SCRIPTURES

Printed in the United States of America

Spirit Media and our logos are trademarks of Spirit Media

🔥 SpiritMedia.US

www.spiritmedia.us
8045 Arco Corporate Dr STE 130
Raleigh, NC 27617
1 (888) 800-3744

Books › Christian Books & Bibles › Christian Living

Paperback ISBN: 979-8-89307-046-0
Hardback ISBN: 979-8-89307-047-7
Audiobook ISBN: 979-8-89307-048-4
eBook ISBN: 979-8-89307-045-3
Library of Congress Control Number: 2024909823

Table of Contents

5 **Vital Truths About LOVE**

I. God loves you unconditionally.

II. You are commanded to love others.

III. You are incapable of loving others on your own.

IV. You can love others with God's love.

V. You love by faith.

L ove is the greatest thing in the world—the greatest privilege and power known to man. Its emphasis in life and word changed the course of history as the first-century Christians demonstrated a quality of life never before witnessed on this earth. The Greeks, Romans, Gentiles, and Jews hated one another. The very idea of love and self-sacrifice was foreign to their thinking. When they observed Christians from many nations, with different languages and cultures, loving one another and sacrificing to help each other, they responded in amazement, "Behold, how these people love one another!" Everybody wants to be loved. Most psychologists agree that man's greatest need is to love and be loved. No barrier can withstand the mighty force of love. There are three Greek words translated into the one English word "love": Eros, which suggests sensual desire; Phileo, which is used for friendship or love of one's friends or relatives—it conveys a sense of loving someone because the individual is worthy of love; and Agape, which is God's love: the purest, deepest kind of love—it is expressed, not through mere emotions, but as an act of one's will.

Agape is God's supernatural, unconditional love for you revealed supremely through our Lord's death on the cross for our sins. It is the supernatural love He wants to produce in you and through you to others, by His Holy Spirit. Agape love is given because of the character of the person loving rather than because of the worthiness of the object of that love. Sometimes it is love "in spite of" rather than "because of."

God underscores the importance of this kind of love through the inspired pen of the apostle Paul, as recorded in 1 Corinthians 13. In this beautiful and remarkable passage of Scripture, Paul writes that, apart from love, anything you might do for God or others is of no value. Consider these words: "If I had the gift of being able to speak in other languages without learning them, and could speak in every language there is in all of heaven and earth, but didn't love others, I would only be making noise." (1 Cor 13:1 TLB)

Sometimes, people may give their lives willingly for ones they deem worthy—a friend, a relative, other "good" people—but Christ's love goes beyond that. Christ's love extends to those least worthy. He willingly took the punishment of those who tortured Him, hated Him, rebelled against Him, and cared nothing about Him, those who were least deserving of His love (See Rom 5:6—8 ESV). He gave the most He could give for those who deserved it the least! Sacrifice, then, is the essence of godly love, agape love. This is God-like love, not human-like love. (See Matt 5:43-48 ESV)

This love, which Jesus demonstrated toward us on the cross, is just the beginning. When we place our trust in Him as our Savior, He makes us God's children, co-heirs with Him! He comes to dwell within us through His Holy Spirit, promising He will never leave us nor forsake us (See Heb 13:5—6, ESV). Thus, we have a loving companion for life. And no matter what we go through, He is there, and His love is ever available to us (See Rom 8:35, ESV). But as He rightfully reigns as a benevolent King in heaven, we need to give Him the position He deserves in our lives as well, that of master and not merely companion. It is only then we will experience life as He intended and live in the fullness of His love. (See John 10:10b ESV)

"If I had the gift of prophecy and knew all about what is going to happen in the future, knew everything about everything, but didn't love others, what good would it do? Even if I had the gift of faith so that I could speak to a mountain and make it move, I would still be worth nothing at all without love." (1 Cor 13:2 TLB)

But what more can we know about agape? How does this kind of love express itself? Paul provides an excellent description in 1 Cor 13:4—8 and 13 (TLB):

> *Love is very patient and kind, never jealous or envious, never boastful, or proud, never haughty, or selfish or rude. Love does not demand its own way. It is not irritable or touchy. It does not hold grudges and will hardly even notice when others do it wrong. It is never glad about injustice, but rejoices whenever truth wins out. If you love someone you will be loyal to him no matter what the cost. You will always believe in him, always expect the best of him, and always stand your ground in defending him. All the special gifts and powers from God will someday come to an end, but love goes on forever...There are three things that remain—faith, hope, and love—and the greatest of these is love.*

In the next chapter, the apostle Paul, inspired by the Holy Spirit, admonishes: "Let love be your greatest aim." (1 Cor 14:1a TLB)

Let us look to the Five Vital Truths About Love that will help you understand the basis for loving by faith.

God
Loves You
Unconditionally

God loves with agape, the love described in 1 Corinthians 13. He loves you so much that He sent His Son to die on the cross for you, that you might have everlasting life. His love is not based on performance. Christ loves you so much that, while you were yet a sinner, He died for you.

God's love for you is unconditional and undeserved. He loves you in spite of your disobedience, your weakness, your sin, and your selfishness. He loves you enough to provide a way to abundant, eternal life. From the cross, Christ cried out, "Father, forgive them for they know not what they do." (See Luke 23:34 TLB) If God loved those who are sinners that much, can you imagine how much He loves you—His child through faith in Christ who seeks to please Him?

Lessons in Love from the Prodigal Son

The parable of the prodigal son, as recorded in Luke 15, illustrates God's unconditional love for His children. Herein, a man's younger son asked his father for his share of the estate, packed his belongings, and took a trip to a distant land where he wasted all his money on parties and worthless wastes. About the time his money was gone, a great famine swept over the land, and he began to starve. He finally came to his senses and realized that his father's hired men at least had food to eat. He decided, "I will go home to my father and say, 'Father, I have sinned against both heaven and you, and am no longer worthy of being called your son. Please take me on as a hired man.'" (See vs. 21 TLB.) While he was still a long distance away, his father saw him coming and was filled with loving pity. He ran to his son, embraced him, and kissed him. I think the reason he saw his son coming, while he was still a long distance away, was because he was praying for his son's return and spent much time each day watching that lonely road on which his son might appear.

Even as the son was making his confession, the father interrupted to instruct the servants to kill the fatted calf and prepare for a celebration—his lost son had repented; he had changed his mind and had returned to become part of the family again.

God demonstrated His love for us before we were Christians, but this story makes it obvious that God continues to love his child who has strayed far from Him. He eagerly awaits his return to the Christian family and fellowship.

Even when you are disobedient, He continues to love you, waiting for you to respond to His love and forgiveness. Paul writes:

Since by his blood he did all this for us as sinners, how much more will he do for us now that He has declared us not guilty? Now he will save us from all of God's wrath to come. And since, when we were his enemies, we were brought back to God by the death of his Son, what blessings he must have for us now that we are his friends, and he is living within us! (Rom 5:9—10 TLB).

God Disciplines the Ones He Loves

The love that God has for you is far beyond our human comprehension. Jesus prayed, "My prayer for all of them [the disciples and believers of all ages] is that they will be of one heart and mind, just as you and I are, Father—that just as you are in me and I am in you, so they will be in us, and the world will believe you sent me." (John 17:21 TLB)

Think of it! God loves you as much as He loves His only begotten Son, the Lord Jesus. What a staggering, overwhelming truth to comprehend! You need have no fear of someone who loves you perfectly. You need never be reluctant to trust God with your entire life, for He truly loves you. And the almost unbelievable part of it is that He loves you even when you are disobedient.

Hebrews 12:5—6a, 7, 9—11 (TLB) teaches about the love that motivates God's discipline:

...have you quite forgotten the encouraging words God spoke to you, his

child? He said, "My son, don't be angry when the Lord punishes you. Don't be discouraged when he has to show you where you are wrong. For when he punishes you, it proves that he loves you... Let God train you, for he is doing what any loving father does for his children. Whoever heard of a son who was never corrected? Since we respect our fathers here on earth, though they punish us, should we not all the more cheerfully submit to God's training so that we can begin to really live? Our earthly fathers trained us for a few brief years, doing the best for us that they knew how, but God's correction is always right and for our best good, that we may share his holiness. Being punished isn't enjoyable while it is happening—it hurts! But afterwards we can see the result, a quiet growth in grace and character.

Christ's death on the cross has once and for all satisfied the wrath and justice of God for the believer's sin. God chastens and disciplines you to help you grow and mature spiritually.

God's Love Reaches Beyond Circumstances

The early Christians endured persecution, hardships, and unbelievable suffering. Yet Paul wrote to them in Romans 8:35—39 (TLB):

Who then can ever keep Christ's love from us? When we have trouble or calamity, when we are hunted down or destroyed, is it because he doesn't love us anymore? And if we are hungry, or penniless, or in danger, or threatened with death, has God deserted us?

No, for the Scriptures tell us that for his sake we must be ready to face death at every moment of the day—we are like sheep awaiting slaughter; but despite all this, overwhelming victory is ours through Christ who loved us enough to die for us. For I am convinced that nothing can ever separate us from his love. Death can't, and life can't. The angels won't, and all the powers of hell itself cannot keep God's love away. Our fears for today, or worries about tomorrow or where we are— high above the sky, or in the deepest ocean—nothing will ever be able to separate us from the love of God demonstrated by our Lord Jesus Christ when he died for us.

Such love is beyond our ability to grasp with our limited minds.

You are Commanded to Love Others

A certain lawyer asked Jesus, "Sir, which is the most important command in the laws of Moses?" (Matt 22:36 TLB).

"Jesus replied, 'Love the Lord your God with all your heart, soul and mind.' This is the first and greatest commandment. The second most important is similar: 'Love your neighbor as much as you love yourself.' All the other commandments and all the demands of the prophets stem from these two laws and are fulfilled if you obey them. Keep only these and you will find that you are obeying all the others" (Matt 22:37—40 TLB).

God's Character and Holy Spirit Motivate Love

First, the Holy Spirit has to fill your heart with God's love, as promised in Romans 5:5 (TLB):

"We know how dearly God loves us, and we feel this warm love everywhere within us because God has given us the Holy Spirit to fill our hearts with His love."

Second, by meditating on the attributes of God and the wonderful things He has done and is doing for you, you then find your love for Him growing. You love Him because He first loved you.

How could God love you so much that He was willing to die for you? Why should God choose you to be His child? By what merit do you deserve to be His ambassador to tell this good news of His love and forgiveness to the world? On what basis do you deserve the privilege of His constant presence and His in-dwelling Spirit, of His promise to supply all your needs according to His riches in glory? Why should you have the privilege—denied to most of the people of the world who do not know our Savior—of waking each morning with a song in your heart and praise to Him on your lips for the love and joy and peace that He so generously gives to all who place their trust in His dear Son, the Lord Jesus? All because of His unconditional agape love.

Loving God Helps Us Love Others

It is natural for you to fulfill the command to love your neighbor as yourself, if you truly love God with all your heart, soul, and mind. If you are properly related to God on the vertical plane, you will be properly related to others on the horizontal plane. When individual Christians are vitally yoked to Christ and related to God and are walking in the Spirit, loving Him with all their hearts, souls, and minds, they will fulfill God's command to love others as themselves.

In Romans 13:9—10 (TLB), the Apostle Paul explains:

> *If you love your neighbor as much as you love yourself you will not want to harm or cheat him, or kill him or steal from him. And you won't sin with his wife or want what is his or do anything else the Ten Commandments say is wrong. All ten are wrapped up in this one, to love your neighbor as you love yourself. Love does no wrong to anyone. That's why it fully satisfies all of God's requirements. It is the only law you need.*

It is love for God and for others that results in righteousness, in fruit, and in glory to Christ. Also, you were commanded to love others because such love testifies to your relationship with the Father. You demonstrate that you belong to Christ by your love for others. The Apostle John practically equates your salvation with the way you love others when he says that if you don't love others, you do not know God, for He is love.

In John 3:17—18 (TLB), we read:

> *But if someone who is supposed to be a Christian has enough money to live well, and sees a brother in need, and won't help him—how can God's love be within him? Little children, let us stop just saying we love people; let us really love them, and show it by our actions.*

Jesus says:

> *"I demand that you love each other as much as I love you." (John 15:2 TLB)*

Viewing Others (and Ourselves) as God's Creations Motivates Love

As a Christian you should love your neighbor because your neighbor is a creature of God made in the image of God; because God loves your neighbor; and because Christ died for your neighbor. Following the example of our Lord, you should love everyone, even as Christ did. You should devote your life to helping others experience His love and forgiveness.

Jesus also said:

> *"There is a saying, 'Love your friends and hate your enemies.' But I say: Love your enemies! Pray for those who persecute you! In that way, you will be acting as true sons of your Father in heaven. For he gives his sunlight to both the evil and the good, and sends rain on the just and on the unjust too. If you love only those who love you, what good is that? Even scoundrels do that much. If you are friendly only to your friends, how are you different from anyone else? Even the heathen do that." (Matt 5:43—47 TLB)*

When Christians begin to act like Christians and love God, their neighbors, their enemies and especially their Christian brothers—regardless of color, race, or class—we will see in our time, as in the first century, a great transformation in the whole of society. People will marvel when they observe our love, in the same way people marveled when they observed those first century believers saying, "Look at how they love one another." (See Tertullian, The Apology, Chapter 39)

Get your eyes off yourself! Focus your love and attention on Christ and on others. Begin to lose yourself in service for Him and for your fellow human beings.

God's kind of love is a unifying force among Christians! Paul admonishes us to "put on love, which is the bond of perfection" (Col 3:14 TLB). Only God's universal love can break through the troublesome barriers that are created by human differences. Only a common devotion to Christ—the source of love—can relieve tension, ease mistrust, encourage openness, bring out the best in people, and enable them to serve Christ together in a more fruitful way.

One mother shared that the discovery of these principles enabled her to be more patient and kind to her husband and children. "The children were driving me out of my mind with all of their childish demands," she confided. "I was irritable with them, and because I was so miserable, I was a critical and nagging wife. No wonder my husband found excuses to work late at the office. It is all different now; God's love permeates our home since I learned how to love by faith."

A husband reported, "My wife and I have fallen in love all over again, and I am actually enjoying working in my office with men whom I couldn't stand before I learned how to love by faith."

You are Incapable of Loving Others on your Own.

Just as surely as "those who are in the flesh [worldly, carnal persons] cannot please God" (Rom 8:8 AMP), so in your own strength you cannot love as you ought.

You cannot demonstrate agape, God's unconditional love for others, through your own efforts. How many times have you resolved to love someone? How often have you tried to manufacture positive, loving emotion toward another person for whom you felt nothing? It is impossible, isn't it? In your own strength, it is not possible to love with God's kind of love.

By nature, people are not patient and kind. We are jealous, envious, and boastful. We are proud, haughty, selfish, and rude, and we demand our own way. We could never love others the way God loves us; this is beyond our ability to experience with our hearts.

CHAPTER 3

If I gave everything I have to poor people, and if I were burned alive for preaching the Gospel but didn't love others, it would be of no value whatever (1 Cor 13:3 TLB).

In other words, no matter what you do for God and for others, it is of no value unless God's love motivates you.

You can Love Others with God's Love

It was God's kind of love that brought you to Christ. It is this kind of love that is able to sustain and encourage you each day. Through His love in you, you can bring others to Christ and minister to fellow believers as God has commanded.

God's love was supremely expressed in the life of Jesus Christ. You have a perfect, complete picture of God's kind of love in the birth, character, teachings, life, death, and resurrection of His Son.

How does this love enter your life? It becomes yours the moment you receive Jesus Christ, and the Holy Spirit comes to indwell your life. In Romans 5:5b (TLB), we read: "We feel this warm love everywhere within us because God has given us the Holy Spirit to fill our hearts with his love." God is Spirit and the "fruit of the Spirit is love..." (Gal 5:22 TLB). When you are controlled by the Spirit, you can love with God's love.

CHAPTER 4

When Christ comes into your life and you become a follower of Jesus, God gives you the resources to be a different kind of person. Along with the motivation, He also gives you the ability. He provides you with a new kind of love.

But how do you make love a practical reality in your life? How do you love? By resolutions? By self-imposed discipline? No. The only way to love is explained in this final point.

You Love
by
Faith

Everything about the Christian life is based on faith. You love by faith just as you received Christ by faith, just as you are filled with the Holy Spirit by faith, and just as you walk by faith. If the fruit of the Spirit is love, you may logically ask, "Is it not enough to be filled with the Spirit?" This will be true from God's point of view, but it will not always be true in your actual experience.

Demonstrating God's Love Requires Faith

Many Christians have loved with God's love and have demonstrated the fruit of the Spirit in their lives without consciously or specifically claiming His love by faith. Yet, without being aware of the fact, they were indeed loving by faith; therefore, they did not find it necessary to claim God's love by faith as a specific act.

In Hebrews 11:6 (ESV) we read, "without faith it is impossible to please Him." Obviously, there will be no demonstration of God's love where there is no faith.

If you have difficulty in loving others, remember that Jesus has commanded us to love each other as He loves us. It is God's will for you to love. He would not command you to do something that He will not enable you to do. In 1 John 5:14 and 15, God promises that if you ask anything according to His will, He hears and answers you. Relating this promise to God's command, you can claim by faith the privilege of loving with His love.

God has an unending supply of His divine, supernatural, agape love for you. It is for you to claim, to grow on, to spread to others, and thus to reach hundreds and thousands with the love that counts, the love that will bring them to Jesus Christ.

In order to experience and share this love, you must claim it by faith; that is, trust His promise that He will give you all that you need to do His will because of His command and promise.

This truth is not new. It has been recorded in God's Word for two thousand years. When you begin to practice loving by faith, you will find that problems of tension with other individuals seem to disappear, often miraculously.

Two Attorneys Turn from Hate to Love

Two gifted attorneys had great professional animosity, even hatred, one for the other. Even though they were distinguished members of the same firm, they were constantly criticizing and making life miserable for each other.

One of the men received Christ and, some months later, went to his pastor for counsel and told him: "I have hated and criticized my partner for years, and he has been equally antagonistic toward me. But now that I am a Christian, I don't feel right about continuing our warfare. What shall I do?"

"Why not ask your partner to forgive you and tell him that you love him?" the Pastor suggested.

"I could never do that!" he exclaimed. "That would be hypocritical. I don't love him. How could I tell him I love him when I don't?"

The Pastor explained that God commands His children to love even their enemies and that His agape, supernatural, unconditional love is an expression of our will which we exercise by faith.

He said the 1 Corinthians 13 kind of love is:

... very patient and kind, never jealous or envious, never boastful, or proud, never haughty, or selfish or rude. Love does not demand its own way. It is not irritable or touchy. It does not hold grudges and will hardly even notice when others do it wrong. It is never glad about injustice, but rejoices whenever truth wins out. If you love someone you

will be loyal to him no matter what the cost. You will always believe in him, always expect the best of him, and always stand your ground in defending him. (1 Cor 13:4—7 TLB).

"You will note," the Pastor explained, "that each of these descriptions of love is not an expression of the emotions, but of the will."

Together the lawyer and the Pastor knelt to pray and the lawyer asked God's forgiveness for his critical attitude toward his law partner and claimed God's love for him by faith.

Early the next morning, this Christian lawyer walked into his partner's office and announced, "Something wonderful has happened to me. I have become a Christian. And I have come to ask you to forgive me for all that I have done to hurt you in the past and to tell you that I love you."

His partner was so surprised and convicted of his own sin that he responded to this amazing confession by asking the other lawyer to forgive him. Then to that lawyer's surprise, his partner said, "I would like to become a Christian, too. Would you show me what I need to do?"

After learning how through the Five Spiritual Laws, they knelt together to pray. Then they both went to the Pastor to tell him of this marvelous miracle of God's love.

The Greatest Power Has Changed History

Today, God is bringing back to our remembrance the biblical wedding of faith and love. Through faith, that supernatural, divine love of God will reach out where nothing else can go to capture men and women for Christ. The love which results from that faith will captivate people everywhere so that, as we live and love by faith, we will spread God's love throughout the world. This love is contagious, attractive, and aggressive. It creates hunger for God. It is active, constantly looking for loving things to do, people to uplift, and lives to change.

The Story of Leonard

Leonard is an example. The night he received Christ as his personal Savior, his heart was filled with love, and a great change came over him. Until then, he had hated everyone and everything.

Often, when he came home drunk at night, he would kick his dog to get him off the porch. In the process, the dog would bark, growl, and try to bite him. Reeling and rocking under the influence of alcohol, Leonard would chase the dog around the table outside.

Soon, his wife would get into the fray. They would curse each other and fight. Eventually, he would kick the dog off the porch, scattering chairs, and flower pots in all directions.

"But the night I received Christ," he relates, "I was so filled with love I think even the dog sensed I was different. He raised himself on his belly and crawled toward me, then lay down on the same feet that had kicked him all the other nights. Take the step: love by faith.

Compassionate Love

A teacher was assigned to work with a hospitalized school child on nouns and adverbs. Arriving at the hospital, the teacher was taken to the burn unit. She had to put on sterile attire, and she found the schoolboy in pain. The teacher felt apprehensive, but she told the boy, "I am the special visiting hospital teacher, and your class teacher sent me to help you with your nouns and adverbs." She went through the lessons' material with him and then left, feeling little had been accomplished. The next morning, when she returned, the nurse met her and said, "Since you were here yesterday his whole attitude has changed. He's fighting back to gain a cure, responding to treatment. It's as though he's decided to live and return to school." WHAT HAD HAPPENED? The boy himself later explained: "They wouldn't send a special teacher to work on nouns and adverbs with a dying boy, now, would they?" Sometimes we impart hope to others by just showing up with love and compassion, and doing what we can in the name of Jesus Christ. When we do what we can, He will bless what we do and all we do. Small acts. To love the Lord is to follow Him wherever He leads, to obey Him whatever He asks, and to trust Him whatever the trial. To love Jesus is to reflect the love God has for us, for "this is love: not that we loved God, but that he loved us and sent his Son." (1 John 4:10 ESV). To love the Lord is to care for the ones He loves (1 John 4:19 ESV; see also John 21:16).

Agape is not based on emotion but on the will. Each characteristic of agape is a deliberate choice to act in a certain manner. Thus, when Jesus said, "If you love me, you will keep my commandments" (John 14:15 ESV), He was teaching that loving Him would be a demonstrable action, not an emotional feeling. If Jesus is to be loved as He commanded, then a conscious choice must be made to act according to the pattern described in 1 Corinthiians 13. Jesus was clear that loving Him is a service (John 14:15, 21, 23, 28 ESV) and disobedience is evidence of a lack of love (John 14:24 ESV). Therefore, to love Jesus is to willfully act in such a way that our devotion to Him is proved through our actions toward Him and our obedience of Him.

Practical Steps to Making Love a Reality

Agape love frequently expresses itself as a flow of compassion. Jesus said, "Rivers of living water shall flow from the inmost being of anyone who believes in me" (John 7:38 TLB). Compassion is one of these rivers. It is a gentle stream of tenderness and concern for another person's needs. Such love compelled Jesus to feed the hungry, comfort the sorrowing, heal the sick, teach the multitude, and raise the dead.

Most of us, at some time in our lives, have experienced this flow of love toward someone.

Perhaps you felt it while washing the dishes, or while working on the job, or driving down the freeway, or sitting in a classroom. You couldn't explain it, but your impulse was to do something special for another person.

What does the Bible say about love?

The Bible says that love motivated God to save the world (See John 3:16 ESV). God's love is best seen in the sacrifice of Christ on our behalf (See 1 John 4:9 ESV). And God's love does not require us to be "worthy" to receive it; His love is truly benevolent and gracious: "God demonstrates his own love for us in this: While we were still sinners, Christ died for us." (Rom 5:8 ESV)

The Bible says that, since true love is part of God's nature, God is the source of love. He is the initiator of a loving relationship with us. Any love we have for God is simply a response to His sacrificial love for us: "This is love: not that we loved God, but that he loved us and sent his Son as an atoning sacrifice for our sins." (1 John 4:10 ESV) Our human understanding of love is flawed, weak, and incomplete, but the more we look at Jesus, the better we understand true love.

The Bible says that God's love for us in Christ has resulted in our being brought into His family: "See what great love the Father has lavished on us, that we should be called children of God! And that is what we are!" (1 John 3:1 ESV). Just as the father in the parable showed love to his prodigal son (See Luke 14:11—32 ESV), so our Heavenly Father receives us with joy when we come to Him in faith. He makes us accepted in the beloved (See Eph 1:6 KJV).

The Bible says we are to love others the way God loves us. We are to love the family of God (See 1 Pet 2:17 ESV). We are to love our enemies—that is, we are to actively seek what is best for them (See Matt 5:44 ESV). Husbands are to love their wives as Christ loves the church (See Eph 5:25 ESV). As we show benevolent, selfless love, we reflect God's love to a lost and dying world. "We love because he first loved us." (1 John 4:19 ESV)

The Bible says our love for God is related to our obedience to Him: "For this is the love of God, that we keep his commandments: and his commandments are not burdensome." (1 John 5:3 ESV cf. John 14:15 ESV) We serve

God out of love for Him. And God's love for us enables us to obey Him freely, without the burden of guilt or the fear of punishment.

In 1 John 4:18 (ESV) we read: "perfect love drives out fear" (this is again the word agape). The dismissal of the fear of condemnation is one of the main functions of God's love. The person without Christ is under judgment and has plenty to fear (See John 3:18 ESV), but once a person is in Christ, the fear of judgment is gone. Part of understanding the love of God is knowing that God's judgment fell on Jesus at the cross so we can be spared. Jesus described Himself as the Savior: "God did not send his Son into the world to condemn the world, but in order that the world might be saved through him." (John 3:17 ESV) The very next verse reminds us that the only person who must fear judgment is the one who rejects Jesus Christ.

The Bible says that nothing can separate the believer from the love of God in Christ (See Rom 8:38–19 ESV). God's love does not wax and wane; it is not a fickle, emotional sensation. God's love for sinners is why Christ died on the cross. God's love for those who trust in Christ is why He holds them in His hand and promises never to let them go (See John 10:29 ESV).

Start Asking God How to Love by Faith

YOU are encouraged to take the first step; start loving by faith and follow that flow. It is God's compassion streaming toward the one in need. The tug of love within you means that He is filling you with godly compassion and that He has chosen you to minister to that individual.

Ask God to manifest His tender compassion through you in some way today. As you pray, ask Him to lay someone on your heart. When you sense God's love flowing through you to that individual, find out his need and begin ministering to that need. By following the leading of God's Spirit, you can help those whom the Lord has prepared for His transforming touch, and you will become part of His miraculous provision. When God leads you to help someone, He will enable you to do what He leads you to do.

A Japanese magazine has a picture of a butterfly on one of its pages. Its color is a dull gray until warmed by one's hand. The touch of a hand causes the special inks in the printing to react, and the dull gray is transformed into a flashing rainbow of color.

What other things can be thus changed by the warmth of your interest and agape love? Your family? Your church? Your city? This hurting world is hungry for the touch of someone who cares—who really cares! Through God's agape kind of love, you can be that someone.

Make a List of Those Who are Difficult to Love

But what about those who seem unlikable? People with whom you may have difficulty getting along? Individuals whose attitudes rub you the wrong way? You are encouraged to make a list of people you do not like and begin to love them by faith.

Perhaps you will place yourself on the list. Have you thought of applying the truths of 1 Corinthians 13 to yourself by faith? Ask God to help you see yourself as He sees you. You have no reason to dislike yourself when your Creator has already forgiven you and demonstrated his unconditional love by dying for you!

If Christ is in you, you are complete because Christ Himself is perfect love, perfect peace, perfect patience, perfect kindness. He is all goodness, and He is in you! Whenever Satan tries to attack you by reminding you of sins which you have already confessed or by magnifying your weaknesses and shortcomings, claim in faith the forgiveness and righteousness of God, and thank Him that, on the authority of His Word, you do not have to be intimidated by Satan's accusation.

Thank God that you are His child and that your sins are forgiven. Thank God, that Satan has no control over you except that which is allowed by God. Then cast this care on the Lord as we are commanded to do in 1 Peter 5:7.

Perhaps your boss, a fellow employee, your spouse, your children or your father or mother is on the list of those whom you will love by faith. Pray for each person. Ask the Holy Spirit to fill you with Christ's love for all of them. Then, seek to meet with them as you draw upon God's limitless inexhaustible, overwhelming love for them by faith. Expect God to work through you! Watch Him use your smile, your words, your patience to express His love for each individual.

Love by faith every one of your "enemies"—everyone who angers you, ignores you, bores you or frustrates you. People are waiting to be loved with God's love.

A homemaker who, through a long cold winter, had seen her family through mumps, measles, a broken nose, three new teeth for the baby and countless other difficulties, reached the point where these pressures and demands became too much for her. Finally, on her knees, she began to protest, "Oh Lord! I have so much to do!" But imagine her surprise when she heard herself say, "Oh Lord! I have so much to love!" You will never run out of opportunities to love by faith.

Remember, the agape kind of love is an act of the will, not simply an emotion. You love by faith. By faith, you can claim God's love step by step, person by person.

"The fruit of the Spirit is love..." (See Gal 5:22 TLB). Like fruit, love grows. Producing fruit requires a seed, then a flower, then pollination, then warm sun, and refreshing rains, and even some contrary winds. Similarly, in daily life, your love will be warmed by joy, watered by tears, and spread by the winds of circumstances.

God uses all that you experience to work His will in your life. He is the one who makes your love grow. It is a continual, ever-increasing process. As Paul says, *"May the Lord make your love to grow and overflow to each other and to everyone else..." (1 Thess 3:12 TLB).*

Let Love Motivate You

Now, how does loving by faith motivate you to engage in aggressive personal evangelism and contribute to the fulfillment of the Great Commission?

When you begin to truly love God by faith with all your heart, soul, mind, and strength and to love your neighbor as yourself, you will begin to see other persons as God sees them—as individuals of great worth, as those for whom Christ died. As a result, we shall be motivated by the same love which constrained the apostle Paul who said, *"Everywhere we go we talk about Christ to all who will listen." (Col 1:28 TLB)*

Love, God's kind of love, causes the Great Commission to become a personal responsibility and privilege. When non-Christians observe believers not only saying that they love one another, but also proving it by their actions, they, like their first-century counterparts, will marvel at "how they love one another" and will be drawn to receive and worship our Savior with us.

The Bible Clearly Teaches of the Pure Love

"Hatred stirs up dissension, but love covers all transgressions." (Prov 10:12 NET)

"Better a meal of vegetables where there is love than a fattened ox where there is hatred." (Prov 15:17 NET)

"No one has greater love than this – that one lays down his life for his friends." (John 15:13 NET)

"Love does no wrong to a neighbor. Therefore love is the fulfillment of the law." (Rom 13:10 NET)

"For you were called to freedom, brothers and sisters; only do not use your freedom as an opportunity to indulge your flesh, but through love serve one another." (Gal 5:13 NET)

"that Christ may dwell in your hearts through faith, so that, because you have been rooted and grounded in love," (Eph 3:17 NET)

"And live in love, just as Christ also loved us and gave himself for us, a sacrificial and fragrant offering to God." (Eph 5:2 NET)

"I give you a new commandment – to love one another. Just as I have loved you, you also are to love one another." (John 13:34 NET)

"My commandment is this – to love one another just as I have loved you." (John 15:12 NET)

"Dear friends, let us love one another, because love is from God, and everyone who loves has been fathered by God and knows God." (1 John 4:7 NET)

"If anyone says "I love God" and yet hates his fellow Christian, he is a liar, because the one who does not love his fellow Christian whom he has seen cannot love God whom he has not seen." (1 John 4:20—21 NET)

Claim this Love by Faith

How exciting it is to have such a dynamic, joyful force available to us! And it all comes from our loving Savior, Jesus Christ, who explicitly promises in His Word all that you need. You need not guess, nor hope, nor wish. You can claim this love by faith, right now, on the basis of God's command to love and His promise to answer whenever you pray for anything according to His will.

The Bible is full of great verses and passages about the topic of love. God's love for us is a perfect example and starting place to study love. There are also great verses about love in relation to marriage, brotherly love or friendship, and loving your neighbor. Here is a collection of some of the greatest love quotes from the Bible.

More of God's Love Scriptures

There should be no talk of love in the Bible without covering God's love for each of us. This is the love that has led to a path for eternal life. Praise God!

"For God so loved the world, that he gave his only Son, that whoever believes in him should not perish but have eternal life." (John 3:16 ESV)

"But God shows his great love for us in that while we were still sinners, Christ died for us." (Rom 5:8 ESV)

"No, in all these things we are more than conquerors through him who loved us. For I am sure that neither death nor life, nor angels nor rulers, nor things present nor things to come, nor powers, nor height nor depth, nor anything else in all creation, will be able to separate us from the love of God in Christ Jesus our Lord." (Rom 8:37—39 ESV)

"I have been crucified with Christ. It is no longer I who live, but Christ who lives in me. And the life I now live in the flesh I live by faith in the Son of God, who loved me and gave himself for me." (Gal 2:20 ESV)

"See what kind of love the Father has given to us, that we should be called children of God; and so, we are. The reason why the world does not know us is that it did not know him." (1 John 3:1 ESV)

Love One Another Bible Verses

"Owe no one anything, except to love each other, for the one who loves another has fulfilled the law." (Rom 13:8 ESV)

"For you were called to freedom, brothers. Only do not use your freedom as an opportunity for the flesh, but through love serve one another." (Gal 5:13 ESV)

"with all humility and gentleness, with patience, bearing with one another in love." (Eph 4:2 ESV)

"Having purified your souls by your obedience to the truth for a sincere brotherly love, love one another earnestly from a pure heart." (1 Pet 1:22 ESV)

"Beloved, let us love one another, for love is from God, and whoever loves has been born of God and knows God." (1 John 4:7 ESV)

"Owe no one anything, except to love each other, for the one who loves another has fulfilled the law." (Rom 13:8 ESV)

"For you were called to freedom, brothers. Only do not use your freedom as an opportunity for the flesh, but through love serve one another." (Gal 5:13 ESV)

"With all humility and gentleness, with patience, bearing with one another in love." (Eph 4:2 ESV)

"Having purified your souls by your obedience to the truth for a sincere brotherly love, love one another earnestly from a pure heart."
(1 Pet 1:22 ESV)

"Beloved, let us love one another, for love is from God, and whoever loves has been born of God and knows God." (1 John 4:7 ESV)

What Did Jesus Say About Love

"You have heard that it was said, 'You shall love your neighbor and hate your enemy.' But I say to you, Love your enemies and pray for those who persecute you, so that you may be sons of your Father who is in heaven. For he makes his sun rise on the evil and on the good, and sends rain on the just and on the unjust. For if you love those who love you, what reward do you have? Do not even the tax collectors do the same? And if you greet only your brothers, what more are you doing than others? Do not even the Gentiles do the same? You therefore must be perfect, as your heavenly Father is perfect." (Matt 5:43—48 ESV).

"No one can serve two masters, for either he will hate the one and love the other, or he will be devoted to the one and despise the other. You cannot serve God and money. Therefore, I tell you, do not be anxious about your life, what you will eat or what you will drink, nor about your body, what you will put on. Is not life more than food, and the body more than clothing?" (Matt 6:24—25 ESV).

"And one of the scribes came up and heard them disputing with one another, and seeing that he answered them well, asked him, 'Which commandment is the most important of all?' Jesus answered, 'The most important is, Hear, O Israel: The Lord our God, the Lord is one. And you shall love the Lord your God with all your heart and with all your soul and with all your mind and with all your strength.'"
(Mark 12:28—30 ESV).

"'Whoever has my commandments and keeps them, he it is who loves me. And he who loves me will be loved by my Father, and I will love him and manifest myself to him.' Judas (not Iscariot) said to him, 'Lord, how is it that you will manifest yourself to us, and not to the world?' Jesus answered him, 'If anyone loves me, he will keep my word, and my Father will love him, and we will come to him and make our home with him. Whoever does not love me does not keep my words. And the word that you hear is not mine but the Father's who sent me."
(John 14:21—24 ESV).

"'As the Father has loved me, so have I loved you. Abide in my love. If you keep my commandments, you will abide in my love, just as I have kept my Father's commandments and abide in his love. These things I have spoken to you, that my joy may be in you, and that your joy may be full. 'This is my commandment, that you love one another as I have loved you. Greater love has no one than this, that someone lays down his life for his friends. You are my friends if you do what I command you. No longer do I call you servants, for the servant does not know what his master is doing; but I have called you friends, for all that I have heard from my Father I have made known to you. You did not choose me, but I chose you and appointed you that you should go and bear

fruit and that your fruit should abide, so that whatever you ask the Father in my name, he may give it to you. These things I command you, so that you will love one another." (John 15:9—17 ESV)

The Love of God is a Biblical Truth

"But if a person isn't loving and kind, it shows that he doesn't know God—for God is love." (1 John 4:8 TLB)

The Need to Study and to Grasp the Love of God is Vital for a Number of Reasons.

I. The love of God is widely accepted, but wrongly understood. As indicated, many people believe in a God of love, who operates according to their definition of love. Those people will be shocked to find themselves spending eternity in hell if they believe a loving God would not condemn anyone to hell. But the error is not just among the nonbelievers, for many Christians also have a very distorted concept of God's love.

II. The love of God is the basis for God's great acts in history. We find the word "lovingkindness" of God repeated after each line of Psalm 136. The Psalm praises God for His lovingkindness for two major acts in history, the creation of the world and the deliverance of Israel from their Egyptian slavery. The prophets of the Old Testament emphasized the love of God during the dark days of Israel's captivity and the New Testament speaks of the love of God in the person and work of Jesus Christ.

In Isaiah, chapter 63, verse 7 (TLB), we read: "I will tell of the loving-kindnesses of God. I will praise him for all he has done; I will rejoice in his great goodness to Israel, which he has granted in accordance with his mercy and love."

"Call to me and I will answer you, and will tell you great and hidden things that you have not known." (Jer 33:3 ESV)

"When Israel was a child, I loved him, and out of Egypt I called my son." (Hos 11:1 ESV)

III. The love of God is the cause, the basis and the standard for the love we are expected to demonstrate in our lives as Christians.

"You have heard that it was said, 'You shall love your neighbor and hate your enemy.' But I say to you, Love your enemies and pray for those who persecute you, so that you may be sons of your Father who is in heaven. For he makes his sun rise on the evil and on the good, and sends rain on the just and on the unjust. For if you love those who love you, what reward do you have? Do not even the tax collectors do the same? And if you greet only your brothers, what more are you doing than others? Do not even the Gentiles do the same? You therefore must be perfect, as your heavenly Father is perfect." (Matt 5:43—48 ESV)

"If you abide in me, and my words abide in you, ask whatever you wish, and it will be done for you. 8By this my Father is glorified, that you bear much fruit and so prove to be my disciples. As the Father has loved me, so have I loved you. Abide in my love. If you keep my commandments, you will abide in my love, just as I have kept my

Father's commandments and abide in his love. These things I have spoken to you, that my joy may be in you, and that your joy may be full.

"This is my commandment, that you love one another as I have loved you." (John 15:7—12 ESV)

"By this it is evident who are the children of God, and who are the children of the devil: whoever does not practice righteousness is not of God, nor is the one who does not love his brother. For this is the message that you have heard from the beginning, that we should love one another." (1 John 3:10—11 ESV)

IV. The entire Old Testament law can be summed up in terms of love. The commands of the Law; given to the people of God, can be summed up as: love God, and love your neighbor.

"But when the Pharisees heard that He had put the Sadducees to silence, they gathered themselves together. And one of them, a lawyer, asked Him a question, testing Him, 'Teacher, which is the great commandment in the law?' And He said to him, 'You shall love the Lord your God with all your heart, and with all your soul, and with all your mind. This is the great and foremost commandment. The second is like it, You shall love your neighbor as yourself. On these two commandments depend the whole law and the Prophets.'"
(Matt 23:34—40 ESV)

"Owe no man anything except to love one another: for he who loves his neighbor has fulfilled the law. For the commandments, 'You shall not commit adultery, You shall not murder, You shall not steal, You shall

not bear false witness, You shall not covet,' and any other command-ment are summed up in this word, 'You shall love your neighbour as yourself.' Love does no wrong to a neighbour; therefore love is the fulfilling of the law." (Rom 13:8—10 ESV)

V. Love is to be a principal goal ofour lives as Christians.

> *"But earnestly desire the higher gifts. And I will show you a still more excellent way." (1 Cor 12:31 ESV)*

> *"And now these three remain: faith, hope, and love. But the greatest of these is love." (1 Cor 13:13 ESV)*

> *"Pursue love and be eager for the spiritual gifts, especially that you may prophesy." (1 Cor 14:1 ESV)*

> *"And godliness with brotherly affection; and brotherly affection with love." (2 Pet 1:7 ESV)*

VI. It is the love of Christ which controls us.

> *"For the love of Christ controls us, since we have concluded this, that Christ died for all; therefore all have died." (2 Cor 5:14 ESV)*

VII. What we love is what we will tend to be like, to imitate.

> *"Like grapes in the wilderness, I found Israel, Like the first fig on the fig tree in its first season. But they came to Baal-Peor and consecrated themselves to the thing of shame and became detestable like the thing*

they loved." (Hos 9:10 ESV)

VIII. Love is one of the most prominent terms and concepts in the New Testament.

When our Lord was soon to be arrested and crucified, He spoke to His disciples in what has become known as the Upper Room Discourse concerning the things important to them to know in light of His coming death, burial, resurrection and ascension. Love is at the heart of this section.

> *"If you know these things, blessed are you if you do them."*
> *(John 13:17 ESV)*

> *"Therefore be imitators of God, as beloved children. And walk in love, as Christ loved us and gave himself up for us, a fragrant offering and sacrifice to God." (Eph 5:1—2 ESV)*

> *"Peace be to the brothers, and love with faith, from God the Father*
and
> *the Lord Jesus Christ. Grace be with all who love our Lord Jesus Christ with love incorruptible." (Eph 6:23—24 ESV)*

IX. Love for others is evidence of a true faith, and the absence of love is an indication of a false profession.

> *"The one who says he is in the light but still hates his fellow Christian is still in the darkness. The one who loves his fellow Christian resides*
in
> *the light, and there is no cause for stumbling in him. But the one who*

hates his fellow Christian is in the darkness, walks in the darkness, and does not know where he is going, because the darkness has blinded his eyes." (1 John 2:9—11 NET)

"We know that we have crossed over from death to life because we love our fellow Christians. The one who does not love remains in death. Everyone who hates his fellow Christian is a murderer, and you know that no murderer has eternal life residing in him. We have come to know love by this: that Jesus laid down his life for us; thus we ought to lay down our lives for our fellow Christians. But whoever has the world's possessions and sees his fellow Christian in need and shuts off his compassion against him, how can the love of God reside in such a person?" (1 John 3:14—17 NET).

"If anyone says, 'I love God' and yet hates his fellow Christian, he is a liar, because the one who does not love his fellow Christian whom he has seen cannot love God whom he has not seen. And the commandment we have from him is this: that the one who loves God should love his fellow Christian too." (1 John 4:20—21 NET)

If the New Testament abounds with references to the love of God and the believer's responsibility to demonstrate this same kind of love, the Old Testament references are less frequent.

Characteristics of Divine Love

God's Love is Infinite, Limitless, and Unfathomable

"So as the skies are high above the earth, so his loyal love towers over his faithful followers." (Ps 103:11 NET)

"I will recount the steadfast love of the Lord , the praises of the Lord , according to all that the Lord has granted us, and the great goodness to the house of Israel that he has granted them according to his compassion, according to the abundance of his steadfast love." (Isa 63:7 NET)

"May you have strength to comprehend with all the saints what is the breadth and length and height and depth, 19and to know the love of Christ that surpasses knowledge, that you may be filled with all the fullness of God." (Eph 3:18-19 NET)

For all eternity, we shall ponder the love of God, and never will we fully be able to comprehend it, for His love is infinite.

God's Love is Eternal

> *"Give thanks to the LORD, for he is good, for his steadfast love endures forever. Give thanks to the God of gods, for his steadfast love endures forever. Give thanks to the Lord of lords. for his steadfast love endures forever." (Ps 136:1—3 ESV)*

> *"The Lord appeared to him from far away. I have loved you with an everlasting love; therefore I have continued my faithfulness to you." (Jer 31:3 ESV)*

God's love or lovingkindness is everlasting as expressed in Psalm 136. It endures forever. It is everlasting.

God's Love is Immutable, Changeless

How quickly human love can turn to hate in the divorce court. God's love is not like this. His love is unchanging. As God is immutable, so is His love.

> *"There is no other God like you! You forgive sin and pardon the rebellion of those who remain among your people. You do not remain angry forever, but delight in showing loyal love." (Mic 7:18 NET)*

"You will be loyal to Jacob and extend your loyal love to Abraham, which you promised on oath to our ancestors in ancient times."
(Mic 7:20 NET)

"Every good gift and every perfect gift is from above, coming down from the Father of lights, with whom there is no variation or shadow due to change." (James 1:17 ESV)

God's Love is Holy

Like God, God's love is holy. It is communicated to us through the Holy Spirit.

"And hope does not put us to shame, because God's love has been poured into our hearts through the Holy Spirit who has been given to us."
(Rom 5:5 NET)

God's love is always an expression of God's holiness. It is also directed toward producing holiness in us. God's love seeks to make us holy.

"Even as he chose us in him before the foundation of the world, that we should be holy and blameless before him. In love." (Eph 1:4 NET)

"Husbands, love your wives just as Christ loved the church and gave himself for her to sanctify her by cleansing her with the washing of the water by the word." (Eph 5:25—26 NET)

Many people think God's love is such that He accepts us just as we are, but He cannot accept us this way. He accepts us "in Christ," just as Christ is. God cannot and will not accept our sin. The love of God is not a guarantee that we will not suffer; it is the assurance that whatever sufferings we endure are directed toward making us holy by a God who loves us. If it was necessary for Christ to suffer in order to demonstrate God's love toward us, why would we think our suffering is incompatible with God's love toward us?

> *"I have told you these things so that in me you may have peace. In the world you have trouble and suffering, but take courage. I have conquered the world." (John 16:33 NET)*

God's Love is Sacrificial

God's love is not self-serving but sacrificial. Love comes at a high cost, and the one who loves is the one who willingly pays the price.

> *"For God so loved the world, that he gave his only Son, that whoever believes in him should not perish but have eternal life." (John 3:16 ESV)*

> *"Greater love has no one than this, that someone lay down his life for his friends." (John 15:13 ESV)*

> *"But God commendeth his love toward us, in that, while we were yet sinners, Christ died for us." (Rom 5:8 KJV)*

"I have been crucified with Christ, and it is no longer I who live, but Christ lives in me. So the life I now live in the body, I live because of the faithfulness of the Son of God, who loved me and gave himself for me." (Gal 2:20 NET)

"By this the love of God is revealed in us: that God has sent his one and only Son into the world so that we may live through him. In this is love: not that we have loved God, but that he loved us and sent his Son to be the atoning sacrifice for our sins." (1 John 4:9—10 NET)

Love always has a price tag, and the "lover" is gladly willing to pay the price. From eternity past, God sent His love on us and purposed to save us through the sacrificial death of His Son.

God's Love is Sovereignly Bestowed by Grace

God's love is selective. When a man wants to marry, he chooses the woman he wants to be his wife. He makes a selection. God's love is likewise selective.

"As it is written, "Jacob I loved, but Esau I hated." (Rom 9:13 NET)

"'I have shown love to you,' says the LORD, but you say, 'How have you shown love to us?' 'Esau was Jacob's brother,' the LORD explains, 'yet I chose Jacob and rejected Esau. I turned Esau's mountains into a deserted wasteland and gave his territory to the wild jackals.'" (Mal 1:2—3 NET).

"You did not choose me, but I chose you and appointed you to go and bear fruit, fruit that remains, so that whatever you ask the Father in my name he will give you." (John 15:16 NET)

God's love is not given to human beings because they are lovely. He has chosen to love us in spite of our miserable condition.

"It is not because you were more numerous than all the other peoples that the LORD favored and chose you; for in fact, you were the least numerous of all peoples. Rather it is because of his love for you and his faithfulness to the promise he solemnly vowed to your ancestors that the LORD brought you out with great power, redeeming you from the place of slavery, from the power of Pharaoh king of Egypt." (Deut 7:7—8 NET)

"But God demonstrates his own love for us, in that while we were still sinners, Christ died for us." (Rom 5:8 NET)

We must conclude then that love is a choice—God's choice. God chose to love us above others, not because of anything which we have done, or will do, but He made a choice according to His sovereign grace.

The Love of God is Personal and Individual

God's love is an expression of His goodness towards individual sinners. God's purpose of love, formed before creation.

"For he chose us in Christ before the foundation of the world that we should be holy and blameless before him in love." (Eph 1:4 NET)

"But we ought always to give thanks to God for you, brothers beloved by the Lord, because God chose you as the firstfruits to be saved, through sanctification by the Spirit and belief in the truth." (2 Thess 2:13 NET)

Conclusion

The first and foremost question I must ask you is this: Have you accepted God's gift of love in the person of His Son, Jesus Christ? Jesus is the "beloved Son" of God, in whom God is well pleased (See Matthew 3:17). Because of this, we should "listen to Him." (Matt 17:5)

To accept the sacrificial death of Jesus Christ on the cross of Calvary as God's gift of salvation to you is to enter into His Love. To reject Jesus Christ and attempt to stand before God in your own righteousness is to shun the love of God and to deservedly await eternal punishment. Only those who trust in Jesus Christ can experience and express the love of God. Those who reject the gift of His love in Christ have no claim on His love. The fact is that none of us have any claim on His love, but those who are saved gratefully receive it, and give glory and praise to Him for His grace.

In our witness to a sinful, lost, and dying world, we dare not distort the love of God. God is the One who defines love, not human beings. We must accept God's love as God has defined and expressed it. We dare not rely on God conforming to the distorted perceptions of love to which fallen persons ignorantly cling. We must be careful not to compartmentalize God's love and separate it from His other attributes, or try to evangelize others by appealing only to the love of God. Our Lord did not indicate that we should depend upon the "attraction" of His love, as much as He has indicated that the lost should be compelled by a sense of His righteousness, our sin, and the judgement which awaits sinners.

> *"Nevertheless, I am telling you the truth. It is for your benefit that I go away, because if I don't go away the Counselor will not come to you. If I go, I will send Him to you. When He comes, He will convict the world about sin, righteousness, and judgment: About sin, because they do not believe in Me; about righteousness, because I am going to the Father and you will no longer see Me; and about judgment, because the ruler of this world has been judged." (John 16:7—11 CSB)*

Why not make this prayer your own: Lord, you would never have commanded me to love had You not intended to enable me to do so. Therefore, right now, on the authority of Your commands for me to love and on the authority of Your promise to answer if I asked anything according to Your will, I personally claim Your love—the 1 Corinthians 13 kind of love—for You, for all people, and for myself. Amen.

S. Alfred Cherubim
Senior Pastor
Redeemer Christ Assembly
Brampton
Canada

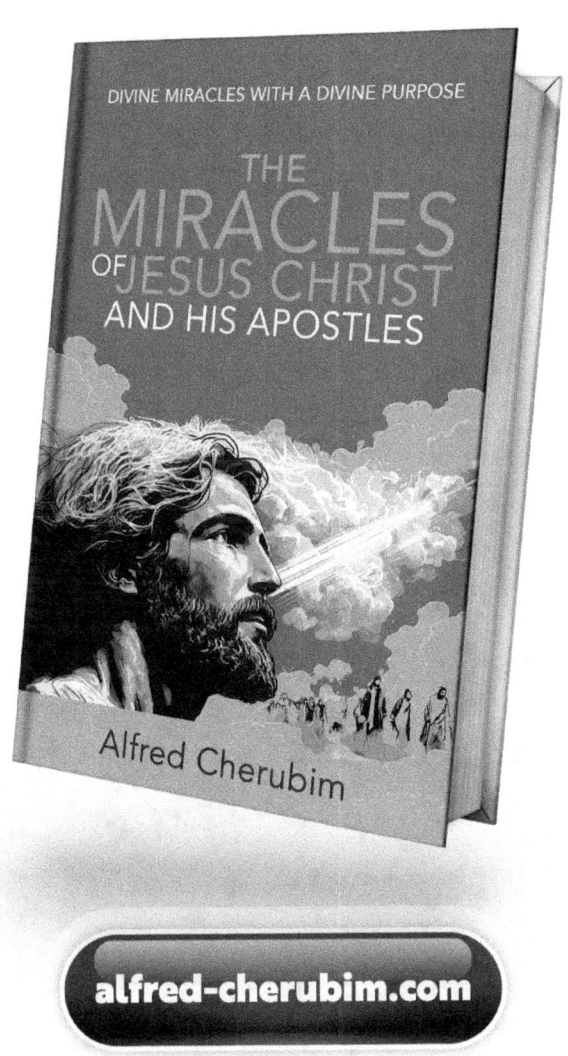

Sharing Your Faith and Testimony
by Pastor Alfred Cherubim

Trusting God Fully and Completely

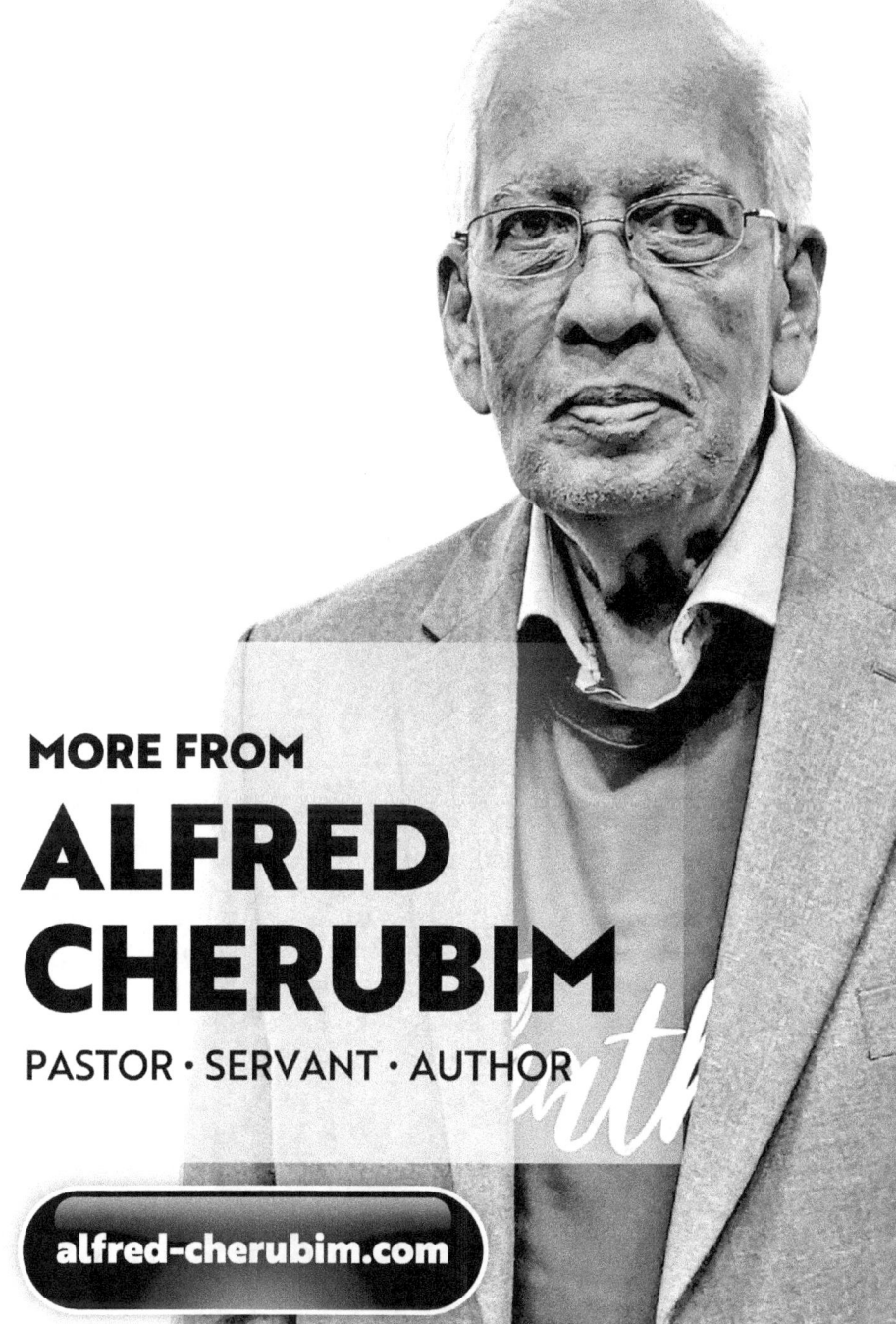

MORE FROM

ALFRED
CHERUBIM

PASTOR · SERVANT · AUTHOR

alfred-cherubim.com